This book is a gift to:

....

....

....

....

....

....

From: ....

Date: ....

MEN-NO-PAWS !

Mr. Lion is wearing the Zulu cross-over bead-wear worn by some men for special ceremonies. Lady Lion is wearing her favourite beaded blanket, the Ndebele married woman's traditional outer garment for when she is outside her home.

He is perplexed by her 'Don't touch me,' 'No Paws' expression. His paws hang in the balance, just off the tip of her shoulders. They need help, let's be there for them!

It was always a mystery to the family when my mother would jump up from the cosy fireside to fling open the windows, allowing the cold mist of the Vumba Mountains, Zimbabwe to rush into the living room. "That's freezing cold!" we would protest. I can still see her as she would wipe the perspiration from her face saying, "It is so hot and stuffy in here, I can hardly breathe!"

Years later, while on a visit to the USA, Rod and I stood in the Colorado snow catching snowflakes on our tongues. Without warning, a claustrophobic wave of heat engulfed me. I ripped off my scarf and gloves while desperately grappling for the zip of my snow jacket.
How weird! A few more incidents leaving question marks all over my husband's face brought the realization that I had caught the same symptoms as my mother. The hot flash was upon me!

With precious memories of my mother who is now with Jesus, and loving thoughts of my daughters, Tammy and Deborah, who are still too young for this experience, I have written the prescription for this season of life with you in mind.
Live and laugh, this too shall pass!
Mom x x x

This book is dedicated to – Our brave, enduring husbands,
Our families and friends,
And to all women since Eve - GIRLS.....WE CAN DO IT!

Acknowledgments:

Special thanks and acknowledgment to Sue Maas who has worked so hard to turn the written description of each illustration into art form. Not only has she totally captured what I tried to explain in words through numerous emails, but has added her own ideas and special touch. Sue, your anointed work 'makes' the book. Thank you!

Graphics Artist: Jeosafá Vasconcelos

Special thanks to Jeosafá Vasconcelos, a Brazilian teacher at Afrika wa Yesu Bible School, Inhaminga. We searched far and wide to find a graphics artist to do the layout of this book. We needed someone who would pick up our heartbeat, rather than someone who would just 'do the job'. Finally we found the right person; not in the far and wide but down the road right on campus! In spite of him not speaking a word of English, we flowed together very well and had a lot of fun putting these pages together.
Thank you for long hours of dedicated work.

CONTENTS

SECTION ONE:
The Seven Dwarves of Menopause

Snappy
Scratchy
Sweaty
Sleepy
Forgetful
Weepy
Psycho
It's a Jungle Out There!
You Are Special

SECTION TWO:
Common Symptoms Of Menopause

Hot Flush
Tearful
Sick & Tired?
Not in the Moo-ed
Highs and Lows
Touchy
Volatile
Down in the Dumps
No Bluff

SECTION THREE:
All Shapes And Sizes

Big Sighs?
Shape up Your Size

Comfort Food
Hang Ups
No No's!

SECTION FOUR:
Spot The Difference

What Men Want -
What Women Want

SECTION FIVE:
(Men Only) -
Tips And No No's

Male Menopause
No Woman-eyes-ing
No Comment
On Pause
Listen
Handle with Care
Rhino Hide
Touch Therapy

SECTION SIX:
(Ladies Only) -
The Way To His Heart

Through His Stomach
No Flirting!
No Old Bones
Don't Fence Me In

SECTION SEVEN:
Blast From The Past

Keep the Fire Burning
Do the Things you Used to Do
♪ ♫ ♪ ♪ ♫

SECTION EIGHT:
Friends

Lonesome Me
Hang Out With a Friend
Have Fun With Friends
My Forever Friend
The Greatest Is Love!
What a Friend

SECTION NINE:
In Tough Times

Never Give Up
Empty Nest
I Believe I Can Fly

SECTION TEN:
Hakuna Matata

Behold!
Grande Finale!

CONTENTS
SECTION ONE - The Seven Dwarves of Menopause

Scratchy

Snappy

Sleepy

Sweaty

Forgetful

Weepy

Psycho

Snappy

Female hyenas snarl and salivate often. Sometimes at their mates!

"Ggggrrrrrrr snap snap snap!"

"It is better to dwell in the wilderness than with a quarrelsome and angry woman." (Proverbs 21:19)

*Designer Head Dress by the San Bushwoman of Namibia
Bow and Arrow Back-pack from Wilderness World.*

9

Making Up is Not Hard to Do!

Try the 'Three Minute Hug'.

Hold each other for three minutes without letting go – feel your heart
begin to melt no matter how uptight it was.
We never grow too old for a good laugh,
we grow old because we don't laugh!

Never go to sleep without making up

*"And be ye kind one to another, tender hearted, forgiving one
another, even as God for Christ's sake has forgiven you."*
(Ephesians 4:32)

Scratchy

She's tail swishing, clawing mad and try as he may, 'just can't find the right tune to play.

When a cat is scratchy don't wind her up, and remember.......... Never rub a cat up the wrong way!

Say it with Flowers!

"Ointment and perfume rejoice the heart: so doth the sweetness of a man's friend by hearty counsel." (Proverbs 27:9)

Take time for a romantic meal together.

Safari Clothes by Kalahari Safari.

Sweaty

**SWEATY – HOT HIPPO
IN THE PINK**

Did you know.............?

a) Hippos secrete a pinkish substance to protect their skin from the sun. This is nature's own sun lotion.

c) In Northern Mozambique, the Makua women cover their faces with a white paste made from the roots of the nciro tree. This keeps their skin soft, cool and clear, preventing sun damage.

Beauty Products from : ZAMBEZI MUD PACKS. Pat onto skin after bath or roll on the banks of the Zambezi river. Cools skin and keeps flies off. Cooling Fan from TREETOP VILLA. Home delivery by Monkey Mail.

Cool Off!

"You are all fair, my love, And there is no spot in you."
(Song of Solomon 4:7)

Sleepy

AFRICAN PAINTED DOGS,
commonly known as Wild Dogs

"Too dog-gone tired to join in the fun!"

Popcorn from *Mielie Machamba
Serving Bowl from Tortoiseshell@roadside.com
Housekeeper hired from *African Dung Beetle Services.

*Mielie Machamba - Corn Field
*African Dung Beetle – A black beetle almost as big as a golf ball. Collects animal dung and rolls it into a ball. Pushes ball for long distances till it reaches home, then lays eggs in the dung ball.

Let Sleeping Dogs Lie!

"Do not stir up nor awaken my love till he pleases." (Song of Solomon 2:7)

IN THE KNOW –
BONE-US TIPS

Finding it hard to be attentive during his favourite show?

i)   Wake up -

ii)   Your man needs a recreational partner to participate in what interests him.

iii) Take an interest in what he enjoys watching.

iv) If it's sport, learn the rules of the game, the names of the players.

v)   If it's Formula One Racing..........get involved and enjoy the ride!

Weepy

CROCODILE TEARS

don't fool nobody!

"You look'n ta see who's watchin' you cry?
Quit yo' crocodile tears honey.
Yo' man's jus' wiped out and worn out wi' yo' cryin'
and he don' know what to do!"

Don't use your oh so easy CROCODILE TEARS ....to manipulate and control those around you.

Krok Dance

Proverbs 15:13 *"A merry heart makes a cheerful countenance: but by sorrow of the heart the spirit is broken."*

Forget the pity party and have a real party

Make a meal of it!

As they say............

"Cry and you cry alone.
Laugh and the whole world laughs with
you!"

 Shoes obtainable from KROKS Tanneries

Forgetful

"Now where did I leave my car keys?!........ store my nuts?!"

 STORAGE CONTAINERS by 'Potty Ladies' of The Clay Potters' Club.

A Senior Moment?

DON'T FORGET TO REMEMBER....... that God loves you and he has forgotten all your mistakes.

WRITE IT DOWN! MAKE A LIST OF THINGS TO REMEMBER

"For I will be merciful to their unrighteousness, and their sins and their iniquities will I remember no more." (Hebrews 8:12)

 NOTEPAD – Biodegradable Dried Bark
QUILL PEN Courtesy of Mr. Nibs of Porcupine Pie.

Psycho
WILDEBEEST IN MIGRATION FRENZY

CAUTION: DO NOT MIGRATE, (ie. leave your husband and kids) because of temporary insanity! This too shall pass!

IN THE KNOW – Every year over 2 million Wildebeest enter into a migration frenzy. Kicking up dust, they mill around, readying for Africa's greatest wildlife spectacle of migration from the short grass plains of the Serengeti into the Masai Mara.

During this period their young have to be kept from the watchful eye of the predators and from crocodiles once they start crossing the river. It is a stressful time of heat and dust, filled with the noise of bellowing and moaning.

***

It is not uncommon for a woman in menopause to think she has lost her mind - only to find that she has!

"For God has not given us the spirit of fear; but of power, and of love, and of a SOUND MIND." (2 Timothy 1:7)

26

Hang In There!

RELAX! CHILL! HANG OUT!

"Thou wilt keep him in perfect peace, whose mind is stayed on thee: because he trusteth in thee." (Isaiah 26:3)

Hammock available from hanginthere@home.net

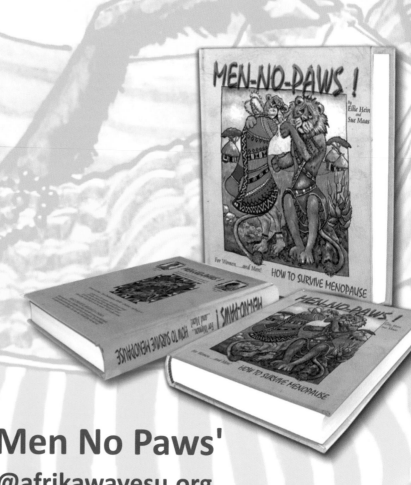

A great read 'Men No Paws'
available from hein@afrikawayesu.org

It's A Jungle Out There!

When you're scared, and you're all alone,
when it's dark and you're far from home
Reach out to God, no need to fear,
Trust in Jesus, He's always near!

"The Lord is my light and my salvation; Whom shall I fear? The Lord is the strength of my life; Of whom shall I be afraid?" (Psalm 27:1)

You Are Special

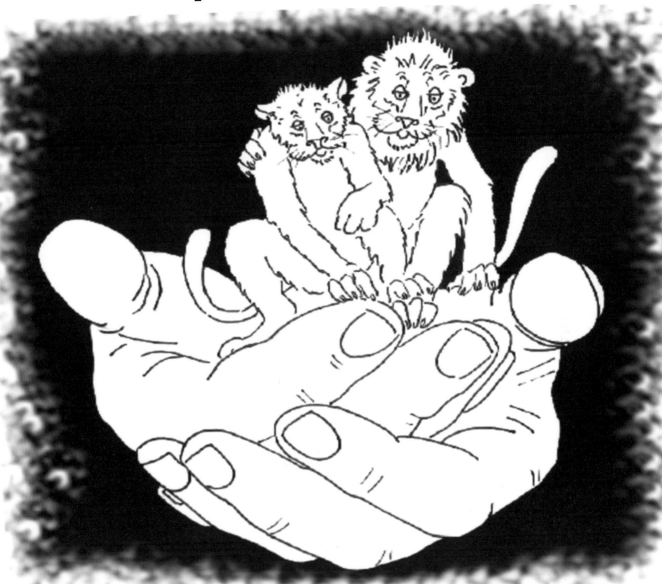

You're God's Chosen Creation!

"I will praise You, for I am fearfully and wonderfully made; Marvellous are Your works, And that my soul knows very well." (Psalm 139:14)

TO THE LAST FINISHING TOUCH!

"Therefore, if anyone is in Christ, he is a new creation; old things have passed away; behold, all things have become new."
(2 Corinthians 5:17)

REGRET NO ORDERS.
Only one of a kind ever produced
Uniquely fashioned by DIVINE LOVE

CONTENTS
SECTION TWO - Common Symptoms of Menopause

Hot Flush

Tearful

Sick & Tired?

Not in the Moo-ed

Highs and Lows

Touchy

Volatile

Down in the Dumps

No Bluff

Hot Flush - one of the earliest symptoms of menopause.

Fill a spray bottle with water and spray yourself. It feels great.

 Nail Polish from Mahogany Pod Tips.
Body Mist can be purchased at 'The Smoke that Thunders', Victoria Falls, Zimbabwe.
Sun Brolly borrowed from tourist by the river.

Sweatmare.

It is not uncommon to wake up several times a night drenched with sweat, even in the middle of winter.

Claustrophobic heat may cause you to throw off the blankets, too desperate to notice hubby is shivering with cold!

Spray Yourself with cool water. Oops! Careful not to spray hubby by mistake!
Chuckle chuckle, "Who said anything about a mistake? ☺"

IN THE KNOW - ABOUT SWEATS
i)   It helps to cut down on caffeine!
ii)   During cold weather - wear layers of clothing you can peel off as required, rather than one thick jacket.

Tearful

The Fact is:

During menopause, woman often cry easily for no reason.

Always have a hankerchief ready.

Remember, this too shall pass.

If possible, go and cry somewhere private.

For Crying Out Loud!

Not such a bad idea.

Get yourself somewhere ALONE and have a good HOWL.

It will bring a therapeutic release deep inside and you will feel much better - and everyone else will too.

Sick & Tired?

Tired......Take a short midday nap.

Leave the TV and get to bed a bit earlier! Napping in front of the TV is not restful.

WE OFTEN LOOK LIKE WE FEEL!

A 20 minute walk a day boosts your energy level. 30 minutes is better.

Stay off sodas and drink more water.

Sick ...tension, anger and unforgiveness raise blood pressure and can result in stroke or heart attack. Even arthritis can be triggered or accentuated by a bitter or broken spirit.

"A merry heart does good like a medicine........ a broken spirit dries up the bones." (Proverbs 17:22)

Be Informed:

Anxiety (worry or fear) causes tightness in the chest, your heart is literally affected. Do not worry yourself sick!

Fear is a killer.
 "… hearts failing them from fear." (Luke 21:26)

Stress - Tension Too Tight? Get off the tight rope before you snap.
Many people have literally fallen off the edge of their mind when things have become too much for them.

Seek help from a Christian friend or counsellor before it's too late.

"Don't assume that you know it all. Run to GOD! Run from evil!
Your body will glow with health, your very bones will vibrate with life!"
(Proverbs 3:7,8) (The Message Translation)

Sin causes sickness?
Get this. After a heated argument or hurtful words, your immune system is lowered for up to 24 hours!!!!!!!!!! This opens the door for catching colds, 'flu, etc.

Forgive, make up and let the life and love flow.
Live in Christ – As you live in Him and the way He wants you to live, you recreate and build up your immune system and are charged with vitality!

"In Him (that is God) we live and move, and have our being." (Acts 17:28)

Laughter Therapy

Laughter releases endorphins (happy hormones) and brings a healing flow into your body.

DID YOU KNOW............... The Best medicine is free?!

- Laughter boosts blood flow by 20% and reduces the risk of heart disease.
- Laughter also helps fight infections and allergies.
- Just 15 minutes of laughter a day helps boost your immune system.
- It increases the amount of immunoglobulius, natural cell killers that fight infection and tumours.
- Laughter eases pain, physical as well as emotional!
- Positive effects of a good laugh lasts for up to 40 minutes!
- Laughter dissolves tension, stress, anxiety, anger, grief and depression.
- **Learn to laugh at yourself!**

GET TICKLED PINK!

Laughter clinics are being established in the secular world to bring health and healing!

Even if you have to force yourself to laugh, it reduces stress levels and helps keep diabetes under control.

Ever wondered why you feel better after a laugh?

Laughter will not only make you feel better, but will help you get better.

Laughter, happiness and joy are perfect antidotes for stress.

YOU TICKLE MY LIVER........literally!

A noted doctor said that the diaphragm, thorax, abdomen, heart, lungs – even the liver – are given a massage during a hearty laugh. Great therapy that can come no other way!

A sense of humour will help you overcome the obstacles of life, rise to a challenge, handle the unexpected with ease and come through difficulties with a smile.

A smile opens doors.

A GOOD LAUGH ONLY! - Cynical, satirical, sarcastic and mocking laughter at someone else's expense is bad laughter. It has the opposite effect in you. It releases negative chemicals into your bloodstream. You can feel the difference by the taste it leaves in your mouth.

HOW OFTEN DO YOU LAUGH? An average young child laughs 300 times a day while the average adult laughs 17 times a day. Adults are too tense, stressed and serious about life. Laughter keeps you young and glowing, puts that sparkle in your eye.
Laughter makes you beautiful!

Positive blocks out negative – To reverse the curse of all these negative feelings and their effects, change from negative to positive and bring health and blessing to your life and those around you. It works!

"Let all bitterness and indignation and wrath (passion, rage, bad temper) and resentment (anger, animosity) and quarreling (brawling, clamor, contention) and slander (evil-speaking, abusive or blasphemous language) be banished from you, with all malice (spite, ill will, or baseness of any kind). And become useful and helpful and kind to one another, tenderhearted (compassionate, understanding, loving-hearted), forgiving one another (readily and freely) as God in Christ forgave you."
(Ephesians 4:31,32) (Amplified Version)

44

Not In The Moo-ed — Headache!

Moo-o- ooo-o — ooooooh ...Ohhhhhhhh moo-oo head!

A woman's sex drive fluctuates erratically during menopause. She can turn instantly from in the mood to not in the mood.

This is dangerous territory, get with it honey. Do all you can to be there for your man.

NB - Keep Reading Men-No-Paws .

In The Mood -Remember that golden oldie?

Music, song and dance will lift your head and put a spring in your step and bring you to life!

A positive mindset and consciously making an effort makes a world of difference.

Moody Blues!

"Aspirin? What for? I dont have a headache!"

Gotcha!

"No headache! Hallelujah!"

Release Tension - Unwind, minimize stress, get happy, be free.

 Lingerie from Silkworm Slip-ins.

IN THE KNOW - Making love often, brings life and togetherness in a marriage.

It will help keep a rocky marriage on course. At all costs avoid shipwreck.

Frequent sex in a loving, intimate relationship has numerous physical and emotional benefits.

Boost your immune system!

When you're in the mood.............you're not thinking of boosting your immune system or maintaining a healthy weight. Yet good sex will do this for you.

Get smart! After sex, production of the hormone prolactin surges. This in turn causes stem cells in the brain to develop new neurons.

On the Other Hand.......Beware of Illicit Sex.

Unfaithfulness does not reap the benefits of loving, pure sex within marriage. In fact, illicit sex has the reverse effect. Living a lie and causing emotional pain and heartache to others will bring down your immune system and open the door to physical, mental and emotional problems; plus broken hearts.

Highs And Lows

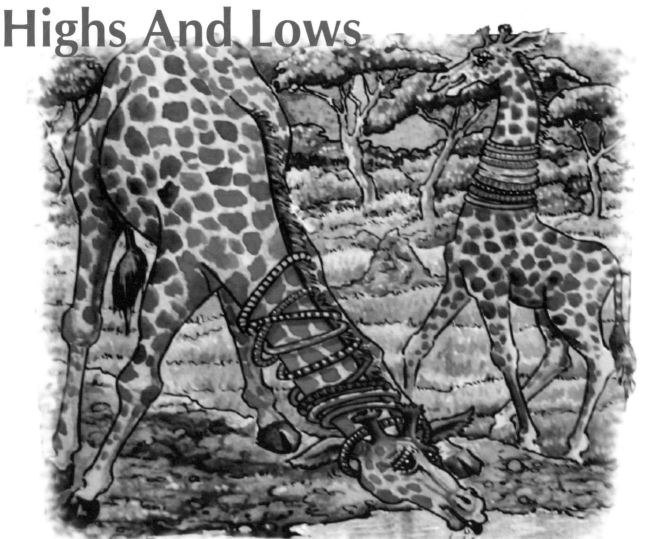

Yo-Yo Emotions & Mood Swings.
Keep Looking Up!

Drink of the Living Water spoken of in John 4:10.
"Jesus answered and said to her, If you knew the gift of God, and who it is that says to you, Give Me to drink, you would have asked of Him, and He would have given you living water."

DID YOU KNOW? Some tribes consider a long neck a great sign of beauty. They wear metal neck bands to stretch the neck. More bands are added as the neck lengthens. If these are suddenly removed all at once, the neck is unable to hold the head. Serious injury or even a broken neck can occur.

Hi's and Lo's are common to women in menopause. Rule your emotions, don't let them rule your life!

"Summing it all up, friends, I'd say you'll do best by filling your minds and meditating on things true, noble, reputable, authentic, compelling, gracious – the best, not the worst; the beautiful, not the ugly; things to praise, not things to curse."
(Philippians 4:8) (The Message Translation)

Neck Bands can be ordered from neck&neck@longneckheights.neck

Touchy?

'What did I do to her this time?'

Try some 'Touch' Therapy

Untouchable?

Lay your Hackles down and try a little tenderness!

TLC (Tender Loving Care) helps the quills lie flat!

Hairstyle by 'TopKnots'

"And blessed is the one who is not offended because of me." (Matthew 11:6)

Volatile

BEWARE of the minefield of pent up emotions.

"And the tongue is a fire, a world of iniquity, an unruly evil, full of poison." (Philippians 4:8)

Watch your tongue! Don't allow hormonal stress to trigger your tongue. For every unkind word spoken, it takes at least 50 kind words to erase the negative effect.

DID YOU KNOW?
Negative emotions drastically affect your stomach. Worry paves the way for ulcers, cysts and even cancers.

If you are unable to release the bottled up emotions inside of you, you could EXPLODE!
High blood pressure can cause stroke and heart attack.

DANGER SIGNS – Continuous knot in the stomach. Tightness in the chest, abnormal acceleration of heartbeat. Lump in throat, drawing hands into fist position.
RELAX - count to ten.

Give the gift of love and forgiveness

The fruit of the Spirit.

Love   Joy   Peace

"How sweet are Your Words to my taste! More than honey to my mouth!" (Psalm 119:103)

Fruit can be picked from the pages of the Book of Life.

"The fruit of the Spirit is love, joy, peace, patience, gentleness, goodness, faith, self control, humility." (Galatians 5:22,23)

Forgiveness releases tension, takes the knot out of your stomach. **Life is short, don't waste it.**

Fill your days with good things from The Tree of Life.

It leaves a good taste in your mouth.

Down In The Dumps.

"Why art thou cast down, oh my soul?" (Psalms 42:5)

"Shake yourself from the dust; arise, sit erect in a dignified place, loose yourself from the bonds of your neck, O captive Daughter of Zion." (Isaiah 52:2) (Amplified Version)

Get up and join in on the fun!

"No flies on me!"

"Wherefore seeing we also are compassed about with so great a cloud of witnesses, let us lay aside every weight, and the sin which doth so easily beset us, and let us run with patience the race that is set before us." (Hebrews 12:1)

Cheer up, you are not alone. The witnesses of God are more than the flies.

Swimwear, and Jewellery by 'Elliegance Fashions'

No Bluff!

Don't live in denial. Get your head out the sand.

Look Up!

Lift your head up high

Face Up to Things,

deal with issues...... trust in God.

"Fear not, for you shall not be ashamed; neither be confounded and depressed, for you shall not be put to shame. For you shall forget the shame of your youth, and you shall not [seriously] remember the reproach of your widowhood any more." (Isaiah 54:4) (Amplified Version.)

Nor will you bear the shame of being single or divorced any longer!

CONTENTS
SECTION THREE - All Shapes and Sizes

Shape Up Your Size

Big Sighs

Comfort Food

Hang Ups

No No's!

Big Sighs

"Mirror, mirror on the wall who's the biggest of us all?"

Big Sighs at your SIZE can make you feel depressed.

It's time to make a decision
for health and happiness and long life.

Shape Up Your Size

Exercise is key to good sex and good sleep – It keeps the heart strong and improves your physique.

Fat and flabby, lazy and lumpy do not bring the energy and enjoyment you need to your nest.

"But I bring my body into subjection: lest that by any means, when I have preached to others, I myself should be disqualified."
(1 Corinthians 9:27)

In The Know - Exercise

like laughing, releases endorphins, (happy hormones)

Walk It Off – Being physically active will help you combat stress as well as those extra rolls. You can diminish anxiety and depression by getting off your be-hind and onto your legs.

You don't have to ride a bike, climb a mountain or work out in the gym. Simply walk briskly for 30 minutes a day. You'll shape up. Your happy hormones will begin to rejoice and you'll feel good!

Comfort Food

Lounging around eating junk food?

WHAT'S EATING YOU?!

Overeating could be triggered by something that's eating YOU! Healthy food will lift you up, give you more energy, make you feel better.

Junk foods will weigh you down.
Stop looking to food for emotional comfort.
Discover the true meaning and purpose for your life.

IN THE KNOW – There are a million weight loss books and remedies on the market. Make it simple by following these simple guidelines.

TO BALANCE THE SCALES IN YOUR FAVOUR
Cut junk and eat a balanced diet
Cut down on anything white , i.e. flour & sugar
Your body needs:
Protein (meat, fish and dairy) for tissue repair and immune system
Carbohydrates (vegetables, fruit, whole grains) for energy
Fats (olive oil, nuts,) for cell renewal and beautiful skin

CUT PORTIONS TO A THIRD - as all unused substances turn to fat.
WATER IS LIFE – Drink lots of it, 8 glasses a day.

Jesus sent the Holy Spirit to be our Comforter. Turn to Him for help.

"And I will ask the Father, and He will give you another Comforter (Counselor, Helper, Strengthener, and Standby), that He may remain with you forever." (John 14:16) (Amplified Version)

Cup Cakes from Calorie Corner
Popcorn from POP Seams
Devil's Food Cake from Guess who?

Hang Ups

Most of us have some of those 'too small' cute little numbers hung away!
Wouldn't you just love to fit into them again? YOU CAN!

Drop A Size ......or Two

Drop a size or two – or three of four, and bring out that cute little number, baby!

Many of your emotional hang-ups will disappear along with excess weight.

You will feel more confident when you are back in your cool clothes.

How's that for style?
It took a while
But it's plain to see,
I am a new ME!

Dress from 'My Own Hanger'
Accessories by 'Delectable Collectables'

No No's!

Mutton Should *not* be
Dressed as Lamb;

Nana Hog cannot pass for
Miss Piggy!

Yes! - Big can be Beautiful!

SIMPLY STUNNING!

Dress stylish not silly.

If you have a large frame with padding that won't budge, You can still be beautiful.

Take care with make – up, colour coding and styles that suit you.

Accept yourself *and* others will accept you.

Be the Best you can Be!

"For you created my inmost being; you knit me together in my mother's womb. I praise you because I am fearfully and wonderfully made; your works are wonderful, I know that full well." (Psalm 139:13,14)

CONTENTS
SECTION FOUR - WHODUNNIT?

The Apple!

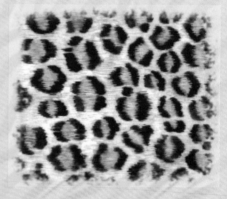

Spot The Difference

Adam ? Eve

The Apple!

Whodunnit?

 Adam   **?**   Eve

"Male and female created He them; and blessed them." (Genesis 5:2)

Ever heard this one?

Adam blamed Eve.
Eve blamed the serpent –
And the serpent ……………didn't have a leg to stand on!

And still we blame one another for the mess the we are in.

It is time to recognize our part in it and REPENT.

"For all have sinned and fall short of the glory of God." (Romans 3:23)

Stop blaming one another for the heartaches in your family.

"For You, Lord, are good, and ready to forgive, And abundant in mercy to all those who call upon You." (Psalm 86:5)

Spot The Difference

Though our basic needs are the same, God created us different,

MALE AND FEMALE

Created He them.

WHAT MEN WANT	versus	WHAT WOMEN WANT
☂ Sex		♀ Affection
☂ Recreation		♀ Conversation
☂ Attractive Spouse		♀ Honesty
☂ Domestic Support		♀ Financial Support
☂ Admiration		♀ Commitment to Family

Understanding one another is half the battle won!

The Ten Commandments Of Marriage

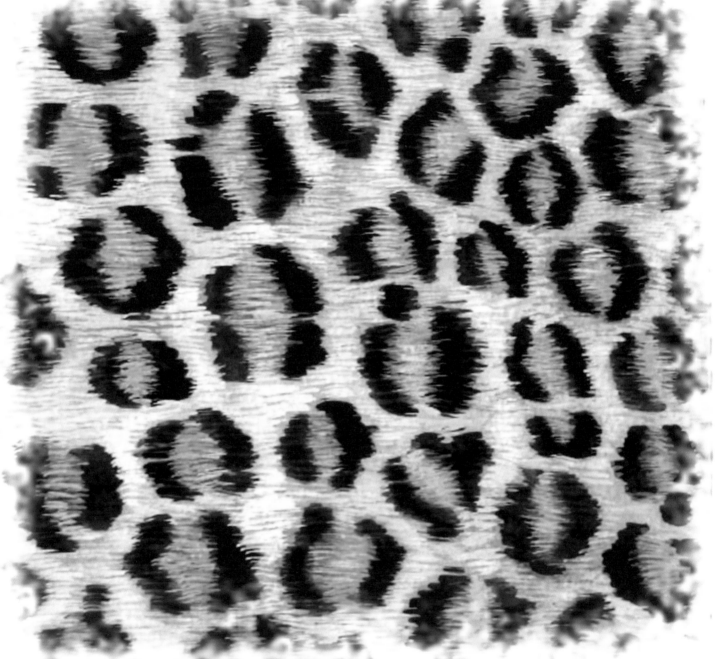

1. Thou shalt have no other mate besides me.
2. Thou shalt not have any image in the likeness of any other but me. Thou shalt not honour nor serve any other but me, for I, thy spouse am a jealous spouse & am likely to kill both the other and thee.
3. Thou shalt not take the name that is ours in vain, for we art joined together as one and it is given forever and is not to be exchanged for another.
4. Remember our wedding date to keep it holy. Six days shalt thou labour and do thy work but the seventh day thou shalt do no work and delight thyself only in me.. Honour me day and night that thou may live long and thy days be happy.
5. Thou shalt not kill the trust between me and thee.
6. Thou shalt not be unfaithful to me thy lawfully wedded spouse.
7. Thou shalt not steal love nor anything thou dost need from elsewhere.
8. Thou shalt never lie to thy spouse for thou shalt surely be found out.
9. Thou shalt not covet thy neighbour's spouse nor covet any other.
10. Thou shall not have eyes for any other, for I thy spouse am a jealous spouse!

"WHAT GOD HAS JOINED TOGETHER LET NO MAN PUT ASUNDER." (Mark 10:9)

CONTENTS
SECTION FIVE - Tips and No No's (Men Only)

Male Menopause

No Woman-eyesing

No Comment

On Pause

Listen

Handle with Care

Rhino Hide

Touch Therapy

No Women-eyesing

Mid Life Cheetah
"OH HONEY, PICK ME, PICK ME!"

Mid Life Cheater

"REJOICE WITH THE WIFE OF YOUR YOUTH" (Proverbs 5:18)

"But remember that the temptations that come into your life are no different from what others experience. And God is faithful. He will keep the temptation from becoming so strong that you can't stand up against it. When you are tempted, he will show you a way out so that you will not give in to it." (1 Corinthians 10:13) (New Living Translation)

"Casting down imaginations, and every high thing that exalteth itself against the knowledge of God, and bringing into captivity every thought to the obedience of Christ." (2 Corinthians 10:5)

 Serpentine Soapstone Carvers of Zimbabwe
Walling by Great Zimbabwe

No Comment!

"You load the cases, I'll bring THE BAG."
Watch your comments, ladies can be very sensitive.

Luggage by Zebraskins

On Pause

'HOLD IT!' – Sometimes you need to put your paws on pause.

Listen

You may not agree or understand, but be all ears anyway!
And do not absent-mindedly say 'Yes Dear.'

Egg Walk

Handle with care. When on thin ice, or walking on eggs, tread carefully - only fools rush in where angels fear to tread!

Rhino Hide

It helps to be thick skinned and have the hide of a rhino!

Try Touch Therapy

Learn how to press her buttons!
Reflexology relaxes tension and brings relief to problem areas.
You'll have her eating out of your hand.

Male Menopause

– commonly known as - MID LIFE CRISIS!

Men-on-pause

If You Can Afford A Harley - Go For It!

But Be Careful –

This is the most dangerous time of your life!
Think more than twice before your trade old faithful for a new model. She may sing and look good, but chances are she'll not see you to the end of your road.

ON ANOTHER SUBJECT

Why do men generally have a shorter life span than woman?
The chief cause of premature death in males is stroke or heart attack. Could it be because many men supress their emotions, not releasing their emotions. Often men think tears are a sign of weakness and do not allow themselves to cry. Guys are taught – "Cowboys don't cry. Especially not in front of the cows!" This is wrong, tears release tension.

IT TAKES A REAL MAN TO CRY. TRY IT.

HE IS A GREAT MAN, WHO HAS NOT LOST THE HEART OF A CHILD.

CONTENTS

SECTION SIX - The Way To His Heart (Ladies Only)

Through His Stomach

No Flirting

No Old Bones

Don't Fence Me In

The Way To His Heart

Through His Stomach

Run Baby Run..................... That's My Dinner, Baby!
Run the extra mile to bring in what he really enjoys.

 Hunting Trips can be booked through hunt@inhamingasafaris.com
Deck Chair of bone and zebra skin from above address.

Make Him Feel Like A King!

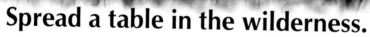

Spread a table in the wilderness.

RECIPE FOR BUSHBUCK

1 Bushbuck from Gorongosa National Park, Mozambique
Rip Belly and remove entrails for hor-d'oeurves
Stuff with snails, wild chili and herbs of the field
Tie up with Buffalo Bean Vines
Sprinkle generously with Mopani Flies
Lay out on tree stump greased with Warthog fat

Decor – Natural Beeswax Candles
Dishes from Tortoiseshell@roadside.com
Vase from The Snailshell Collection
Flowers from Wild@Heart.org

No Flirting!

Undivided attention

Have eyes only for him - he will share you with no other.
Thou shalt not flirt nor play around with other males.

"The heart of her husband safely trusts in her." (Proverbs 31:11)

More Precious Than Rubies

"Who can find a virtuous wife? For her worth is far above rubies.
The heart of her husband safely trusts her; so he will have no lack of gain.
She does him good and not evil all the days of her life."
(Proverbs 31:10,11,12)

Rubies from King Solomon's Mines. Secretly carried from the
Mountains of the Moon
Purse from the Queen of Sheba Collection.

No Old Bones

GET RID OF ALL OLD BONES, old gripes, accusations, negative things of the past.

Let bye-gones be bye-gones.

No more digging up old bones. They STINK!

"Remember ye not the former things, neither consider the things of old." (Isaiah 43:18)

Home Sweet Home

CLEAN DEN - Fragrant and Fresh.

Sweep spider webs from your mind
Get rid of all trash and ugly things
Make up your face with a smile
Place a sparkle in your eyes
Lay out fresh carpet of love grass
Set den temperature at soft and warm
Prepare a fragrant dinner of delicacies
Remember to remove
hare from the stew
Collect drinks from the streams
of living water
Make your den a haven
of love and acceptance.
It's not too late to make
changes in your life.

No matter what has happened in the past, no matter how deep the hurts and disappointments, God can make everything new in your life and in your marriage – if you choose.

"Behold, I will do a new thing; now it shall spring forth; shall ye not know it? I will even make a way in the wilderness, and rivers in the desert." (Isaiah 43:19)

Don't Fence Me In

THAT TRAPPED FEELING is common to man.
If he's snarling and growling and out of sorts - simply let him out.

Freedom!

LET HIM RUN WITH THE BOYS

Men need guy time.
Give him S P A C E

CONTENTS

SECTION SEVEN - Blast From The Past

Keep The Fire Burning

Do The Things You Used To Do

Keep The Fire Burning

Collect your precious memories

Stir up the embers

Blow on them

Mellow yourselves on the sweetness

Reminiscing about the good times helps
to keep the fire burning.

Do The Things You Used To Do

Hire a Harley – Remember the thrill of speed and the open road?

Team Work – Reach for new heights, things look better from up there.

Canoo with yoo? – Cool! BUT do *not* trail your hand in the Zambezi river. A croc could mistake it for a fish. (True!)

Dance with me!

The Couple That Plays Together – Stays Together
Spend time together, have fun together. Do something NEW together!

CONTENTS
SECTION EIGHT - Forever Friends

Lonesome Me

Hang Out With a Friend

What a Friend!

The Greatest is Love

Lonesome Me

LONESOME ME

"Everybody's goin' out and a having fun, ♪ ♫
I'm just a fool for staying home and having none ...... ♪
♫*..Ooooooohhhhhhhhhoooooooooo, Lonesome Me!* ♪ ♫ ♪ ♫

Well there must be some way I can lose these lonesome blues,
Forget about the past and find me.........somebody new."
... ♪ ♫*..Oooooooohhhhhhhhhooooooooo, Lonesome Me!* ♪ ♫ ♪ ♫

"Oh Lonesome Me" - a popular Chet Atkins song, 1958. It reached the Top 10.

Try Jesus, He has promised He will never leave you nor forsake you!

Have Fun With Friends

It is unrealistic to expect your man to meet your every need.

You need chick time!

JUST REMEMBER – While you are on a roller-coaster ride, so are many of your friends . Friendships can be tested and tried during this time, nurture your friendships.

"A man who has friends must himself be friendly, but there is a friend who sticks closer than a brother." (Proverbs 18:24)

"A friend loves at all times." (Proverbs 17:17)

Faithful Friends

Hang Out With a Friend

Need a friend? BE a friend. Your friend needs you during these times!

My Forever Friend

Let your husband be your Best Friend!

"His mouth is most sweet: yea, he is altogether lovely. This is my beloved, and this is my friend." (Song of Solomon 5:16)

 Wedding Rings from Gold Reef City, Johannesburg

The Greatest Is Love!

I Corinthians 13:1-13

If I speak in the tongues of men and of angels, but have not love, I am only a resounding gong or a clanging cymbal.

If I have the gift of prophecy and can fathom all mysteries and all knowledge, and if I have a faith that can move mountains, but have not love, I am nothing.

If I give all I possess to the poor and surrender my body to the flames, but have not love, I gain nothing.

Love is patient, love is kind. It does not envy, it does not boast, it is not proud.

It is not rude, it is not self-seeking, it is not easily angered, it keeps no record of wrongs.

Love does not delight in evil but rejoices with the truth.

It always protects, always trusts, always hopes, always perseveres.

Love never fails. But where there are prophecies, they will cease; where there are tongues, they will be stilled; where there is knowledge, it will pass away.

For we know in part and we prophesy in part, but when perfection comes, the imperfect disappears.

When I was a child, I talked like a child, I thought like a child, I reasoned like a child. When I became a man, I put childish ways behind me.

Now we see but a poor reflection as in a mirror; then we shall see face to face.

Now I know in part; then I shall know fully, even as I am fully known.

And now these three remain: faith, hope and love. But the greatest of these is love.

The Crown He Bore

"Greater love has no one than this, than to lay down one's life for his friends." (John 15:13)

"But God demonstrates His own love toward us, in that while we were still sinners, Christ died for us." (Romans 5:8)

"I owed a debt I could not pay – He paid the debt He did not owe; I needed someone to wash my sins away. And now I sing a brand new song -

AMAZING GRACE!

Christ Jesus paid the debt that I could never pay!"

What a Friend

we have in Jesus!

CONTENTS
SECTION NINE

Never Give Up

Empty Nest

I Believe I Can Fly

Never Give Up!

Keep Trying

We may look a bit worn on the outside, but we don't give up.
Inside we can become more beautiful every day!

"Therefore we do not lose heart. Even though our outward man is perishing, yet the inward man is being renewed day by day." (2 Corinthians 4:16)

Make-Up available from Bushman Paint Shop
Beauty & the Buzzard Brand

Empty Nest?

It's hard when the kids all leave home. This is not the time to mope, but time for fresh fire to come into your marriage.

Allow God to begin something exciting and rewarding in your life – He has plans for you!

"For I know the plans I have for you," says the LORD. "They are plans for good and not for disaster, to give you a future and a hope." (Jeremiah 29:11)

 It may be time to redecorate your nest or even move into a smaller one.

I Believe I Can Fly!

I Believe I Can Touch The Sky!

Psalm 91:1 "He who dwells in the secret place of the Most High shall abide under the shadow of the Almighty."

Psalm 91:4 "He shall cover you with His feathers, and under His wings you shall take refuge."

CONTENTS
SECTION TEN - Hakuna Matata!

Behold

Grande Finale!

BEHOLD

The Lion Of The Tribe Of Judah!

"... and there were loud voices in heaven, saying, The kingdoms of this world have become the kingdoms of our Lord and of His Christ, and He shall reign forever and ever!" (Revelation 11:15)

Grande Finale!

He Will Guide You Through
The No-Paws Path Of Your Life.

Walk in confidence and strength - free to be who you really are!

Invite Jesus to move into your life. Allow Him to rule and reign in your heart. He will fill you with love, joy and peace. Your problems will not all be instantly solved, but as you walk with Him, He will lead you through every trial and heartache and bring healing to you, body, soul and spirit.

It's A Life Or Death Choice - Choose Life!

God is ready to forgive you all your sins. 1 John 1:9
You cannot earn salvation, it is a free gift by faith. Ephesians 2:8
Believe in your heart, Confess with your mouth. Romans 10:9
Believing in Christ is not enough, you need to receive Him also. John 1:12
Salvation is not cheap, it was purchased with His own Blood. Revelation 1:5

Pray this Prayer

"Father God,
                I come to you in Jesus' name.
        How great you are! Before I was born you had a plan for my life. I want to fulfill that plan, I want to be all you designed me to be. I confess I have walked away from you and followed my own way. I choose to forgive those who have hurt me and sinned against me. Please forgive me also. Lord Jesus, thank you for giving your life for me on the cross. Thank you for paying the price for my freedom. Lord, come in to my life, I give myself to you."

John 3:16 "For God so Loved the world that he gave His only begotten Son, that whosoever believes on Him will never die but have eternal Life."

If you have prayed this prayer, be sure to tell someone. Find a Bible-based church filled with the life and joy of the Holy Spirit to attend regularly. It is very important that you meet together with other Christians in order to grow and develope spiritually.

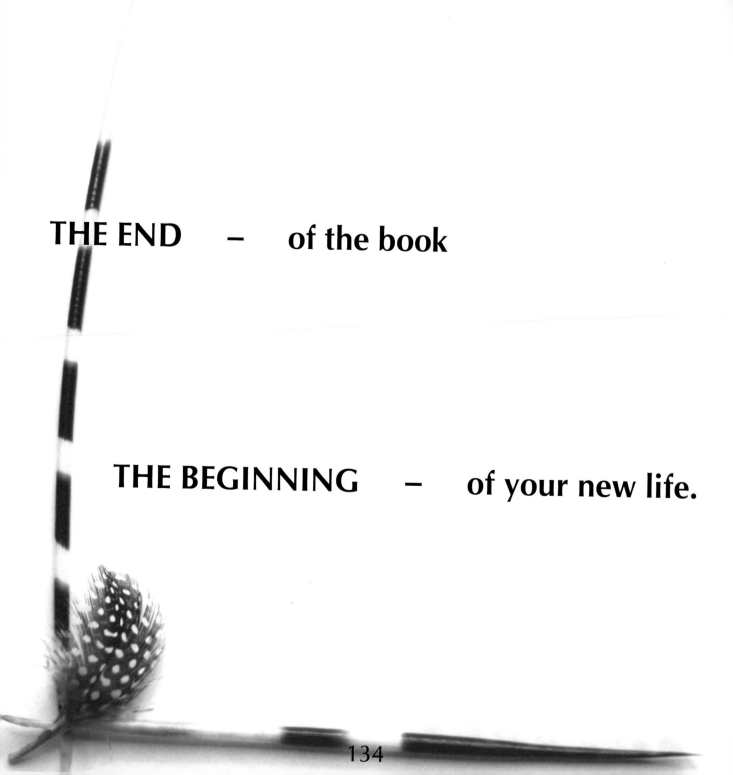

THE END – of the book

THE BEGINNING – of your new life.